Paweł Jankowski

HOW TO SURVIVE IN DIFFICULT TIMES

From the economic crisis to the zombie apocalypse

TABLE OF CONTENTS

AUTHOR'S ODE

I began working on this text in May 2020. The catalyst for its creation was the events surrounding the Covid-19 pandemic, and, above all, the actions of governments that were devastating societies and economies. This prompted me to gather my thoughts and observations about the reality around us, which had been maturing within me for some time, as well as to organize knowledge on how to deal with it all. I do not claim that the solutions proposed here are the only correct path, but experience and intuition suggest to me that following the principles below will allow my family and me to safely navigate the storms of history that surround us. The more than three-year delay in finishing this book clearly demonstrates that much of what I wrote has come true. This gives even more hope that by adhering to the principles below, we will be able to prevail in the upcoming developments. The word "crisis" in Chinese consists of two characters, signifying danger and opportunity. Therefore, I wish for myself and all readers that we effectively avoid the former and maximize the latter, and that we emerge from all of this stronger, wiser, and happier.

INTRODUCTION

The past few decades of prosperity have accustomed us to thinking that this state of bliss will never end. There was, of course, the crisis in 2008, but very few people truly felt its effects, and no one remembers it anymore. Preppers were, of course, preparing for difficult times, but even in the face of the most realistic threats, some of them remain defenseless. What's the use of having a bunker on a plot of land, traps prepared for squirrel hunting, and a van stocked with canned goods for 20 years if the money in my bank account can lose its value overnight, and if I lose my warm job, I can only rely on government benefits? As I write these words in May 2020, the entire world, which has been living peacefully and developing until now, is facing an unprecedented "corona-crisis." Today, most people are aware that the epidemic itself is not the real threat. Rather, it's irresponsible and incompetent people at the top of power and big players who have always caused crises and wars to achieve their private goals. I won't delve into conspiracy theories, of course, because this book is not about that, but I will focus on ways to be prepared for such events and what to do to avoid being crushed by the increasingly faster wheels of history.

WHERE DID MY MONEY GO?

Now, let's get down to the specifics. Every crisis takes a toll on the economy and national budgets. Stock market crashes can lead to the downfall of many banks and corporations. To prevent this, governments resort to printing money to inject into failing institutions. Furthermore, to stay in power, they expand social benefits, thereby increasing public debt. The natural consequence of such actions is rising inflation. As the ancient maxim goes, "history is a teacher of life." So, let's take a look at how this played out in the past. As an example, we'll consider Poland, a country under communist rule for over 50 years.

Starting from the early 1950s, the Polish People's Republic government attempted to stabilize the economy, which was on the verge of collapse due to their earlier ideological moves. The first attempt was the currency reform in 1950. As a result, the communist government confiscated about two-thirds of citizens' savings. Then, they attempted issuing bonds, but that didn't help much either. In January 1953, the communists decided to take more drastic measures. On January 3 of that year, they imposed a top-down price increase on goods and services. Prices skyrocketed overnight by about 100%. Of course, wages were eventually raised too, but only by around 30%, and state propaganda claimed it was all for the good of the working people in towns and villages, and that the reforms were necessary to strike against the "kulaks" (wealthier peasants). From that period, one story has survived in my family.

My grandfather needed money for renovating his apartment. So, he decided to sell a magnificent pre-war German radio. A buyer appeared quite quickly, paid the requested amount, and took his new acquisition. The next day, the money lost so much value that the renovation became unaffordable.

Subsequent inflation spikes occurred in 1982 - 100.8%, 1989 - 251.1%, and 1990 - 585.8%. In the following year, inflation dropped to 70%, and in 2000, it reached 10%. Since then, inflation has generally been on a decreasing trend, and in 2019, it was only 2.3%.

How high will inflation go in [1]2020 and the following years? How can we protect our savings? Unfortunately, first and foremost, we can't escape inflation. As humans, we have to satisfy our immediate needs. So, price increases will affect every consumer. Stockpiling goods may not be the best strategy because we don't know when significant price hikes will occur, and refrigerators and pantries have limited capacity. Instead, let's focus on safeguarding our savings, the funds we set

---

[1] In 2021, according to official statistics, inflation in Poland reached 3.4%. This was the highest result since 2012. In 2022, it had already risen to 14.8%. Let us also remember that official statistics are usually significantly underestimated.

aside for a specific purpose, our financial cushion, or a hedge against an uncertain retirement.

If you have money in a bank deposit, withdraw it as soon as possible. No deposit will protect your money, and currently, [2]banks are even introducing negative interest rates, which means your savings will only shrink. So, where should you invest your savings? Naturally, in assets that have always been a store of value, such as gold and silver. [3]As I write this, the physical prices of these metals are unfortunately quite inflated compared to their market prices. Two factors contribute to this situation. First is the suspension of production at some mints due to the economic freeze. Second is the high demand caused by the uncertain economic situation and inflation threat. Despite the high prices, many people want to invest their savings in silver and gold coins or bars,

---

2   In 2022, the interest rates in Poland were already at 6.7%, but that still doesn't offset the inflation exceeding 14%.

3   In 2021, market and physical prices of metals were relatively aligned, but in the future, they may diverge once again.

realizing that even if they overpay, they may lose less than leaving their savings in local or foreign currency. I personally believe that market and physical metal prices will soon align. Many countries are slowly thawing their economies, various businesses are reopening, and so will mints. Perhaps by the time you read these words, this issue will have been long forgotten. Maybe the corona-crisis is already history, but history has a way of repeating itself, which is why it's worth having precious metals. What should you buy now, silver or gold? In my opinion, silver. While it takes up more space and is heavier than gold, it's currently undervalued compared to historical data. The historical price ratio of silver to gold was around 18 to 1, meaning you could buy 18 ounces of silver for the same price as one ounce of gold. Currently, this price ratio is around 70 to 1. This historical price distortion must eventually move towards equilibrium, and even if it doesn't reach the level it had for most of its history during our lifetimes, it's very likely to return to the 20th-century average, which was around 50 to 1. There are also other reasons to invest in silver, but we'll get into those in the following chapters.

Another good way to preserve the value of your money may be Bitcoin, sometimes called digital gold by some. Many people were put off by cryptocurrencies after the burst of the last Bitcoin bubble. Just as it created many millionaires before, it left many without their life savings after it burst. I'm not here to convince anyone to speculate on cryptocurrencies, but in the current situation, Bitcoin offers significant opportunities for the long-term preservation of invested funds. As I write this, the price of Bitcoin is fluctuating around [4]10,000 dollars,

---

4   In September 2021, the price of Bitcoin was around $45,000. It nearly quintupled in value. By the end of the same year, it even reached close to $70,000 before dropping to $16,000 in the following year. Currently, in August 2023, the price of Bitcoin hovers around $30,000. The price decrease in 2022 was in line with Bitcoin's four-year cycles. According to these cycles, we should expect to see the next peaks at the end of 2025. The price is expected to exceed $100,000 significantly. As you can see, in the long term,

and many experts predict more increases than decreases. Even in the event of significant future declines, it can certainly be said that over time, Bitcoin will rise again, allowing us not only to preserve the purchasing power of our money but also to make a substantial profit.

Another idea for investing your savings is real estate. If you can't afford a house, apartment, or building plot, you could consider a recreational or agricultural plot, or even a garage. Real estate is unlikely to lose value in the long run. Apartments may be an exception, as their prices are currently inflated. However, even if the prices of some properties drop by a few or even several percent, this loss may still be less than the rate of inflation. Moreover, if we don't have to sell them at a low point, they will certainly regain their current value after the crisis. Real estate can also serve as a good safeguard even

---

despite significant price fluctuations, Bitcoin remains a reliable and stable capital investment.

in times of war or occupation. Even occupiers and Germans during World War II respected private property (excluding Jewish assets, of course). Communists were an exception, as they unscrupulously nationalized and confiscated property from rightful owners. However, the takeover of power by communists can be compared to a zombie apocalypse. Nevertheless, as history shows, even during such a cataclysm as World War II and the subsequent communism, property owners, if they survived, retained their rights to their property under international law and could claim their ownership or financial compensation. On the other hand, people with only cash or, worse, government bonds, lost almost everything.

So, what's the best way to invest your savings to avoid losing them? The answer to this question is diversification, which means spreading your savings across different assets. It's also essential to have enough cash on hand to sustain yourself for several months without having to sell your assets in case their value temporarily drops. This will help you avoid selling at a loss during a temporary downturn. So, keep enough cash to survive for at least three months, and invest the rest in precious metals, Bitcoin, and some inexpensive real estate if possible. Ideally, distribute your funds evenly. You can also invest some of your savings in riskier assets, but make sure it's money you can afford to lose. Our primary goal is to preserve the value of our savings, not to attempt to multiply them through risky speculation.

WHAT IF I HAVE NO SAVINGS?

Well, in a sense, you are protected from inflation, but it can make your survival in a difficult situation more challenging. Such a crisis doesn't necessarily have to be a severe global crisis; it can be as simple as losing your current source of income. That's why it's essential to have what we call a financial cushion. Unfortunately, about half of our society finds themselves in this situation. If you're one of them, it's time to change that. How can you do it? There are two ways: reducing your expenses and increasing your income. Combining both will help you build your financial cushion much faster.

Let's start by looking at how to reduce your expenses. The first step is to diagnose where you are spending your money. Try keeping track of all your expenses for a month. Then, analyze your notes and mark those expenses that you consider unnecessary. Calculate how much you could save by cutting them out. Set aside that amount immediately after receiving your income. Transfer it to a separate account or put it in a piggy bank every month. Your goal should be to accumulate enough money to survive for at least three months without any income. To make it easier, you can use some tricks, such as:

Never buy anything on impulse. If you're shopping online, wait one day before making a purchase to see if you still want it.

Attach a note to your wallet and payment card that says, "Do you really need this?"

If you have a credit card, destroy it and set a goal to pay it off as soon as possible. Consumer debt, more than anything else, takes you away from financial security.

HOW CAN YOU INCREASE YOUR INCREASE YOUR INCOME AND PROTECT YOURSELF IN CASE OF JOB LOSS?

If you're working a regular job, the simplest way to increase your income is to ask your boss for a raise. They might refuse, and you won't gain anything, but it's worth a try. However, getting a raise won't necessarily protect you from income loss. Of course, earning more will help you build your financial cushion faster, but having an additional source of income will further increase your security. I'm not suggesting everyone should work two full-time jobs, but it's worth considering if there's a side gig or hobby that can bring in some extra money.

Perhaps you have a hobby that could earn you a few hundred dollars a month? Learning a trade is also a good idea. Offering small craft services can help you earn extra money and, in the event of job loss, combined with your financial cushion, can help you get through tough times. Who knows, maybe over time, you'll build a decent business that frees you from a regular job. The same goes for entrepreneurs. Even if you run a successful business, having an additional income source will provide you with financial liquidity in case your main business hits a rough patch. During the COVID-19 crisis, government actions devastated many industries. Numerous restaurants, hotels, and fitness clubs went out of business. If the owners of these establishments had a second business, their survival would have been much easier. Why is a craft a good idea for an additional income source? Even today, when everything can be bought, skilled craftsmen or artisans have their customers. In the event of a massive catastrophe cutting the world off from mass production, the demand for the work of small craftsmen would instantly rise. In short, someone with a solid craft will most likely not perish.

WHAT IF YOU GET ROBBED?

In challenging times, crime tends to increase. Everyone is trying to survive, and those who don't know how to earn and have no savings are often forced into criminal activities. I grew up in Gdansk in the early 1990s. It was a period of systemic changes and opportunities, in which many people couldn't find their place. At the same time, store shelves were tempting with an unprecedented variety of goods that many couldn't afford. Gdansk was also a popular destination for elderly German tourists back then. So, it's no wonder that "Hilfe, meine Tasche!" (Help, my bag!) could often be heard on the streets. So, what can you do to avoid becoming an easy target for robbers?

Firstly, don't flaunt what you have. In nature, the best defense is camouflage. If you don't look like someone carrying half a kilogram of silver or gold coins in your pocket, you increase your chances of not becoming a robbery target. Valuable items should be carried on your person, not in bags or backpacks, which can be easily snatched. Carrying something truly valuable, it's wise to be in the company of someone else. Two or three people are more challenging targets for a thief than someone moving alone. However, avoiding tempting fate is one thing, and practical defense during an attack is another. How can you defend yourself against an assault?

Firstly, keep your body in good condition. When we are fit, it's easier for us to both escape and fight back. It's a good idea to learn at least the basics of self-defense and develop the appropriate defensive reflexes. Another thing that increases your safety is having some form of weapon. If you're armed, it also boosts your self-confidence. Your potential attacker is likely to notice this, and it's very probable that, like predators in nature, they'll opt for an easier prey. Even if that doesn't happen, having a weapon increases your chances in a confrontation with an assailant.

Of course, owning firearms is subject to numerous restrictions in Poland and many other countries. An exception, at least in Poland at the time I'm writing this, is black powder firearms of separate loading. These include 19th-century caplock revolvers and their practical replicas, which are widely available without the need for permits or registration. Such firearms have a relatively complicated loading process. You need to load powder into each chamber separately, place a projectile, and put a percussion cap with an initiating charge on the nipple behind each chamber. After loading, you can fire six shots from this type of firearm. This system was proven effective in the Wild West and can be useful even today. However, black powder firearms are characterized by their size and weight. While there are pocket-sized pistols and revolvers, the most popular models are quite large and may be better suited for home defense than as concealed carry weapons.

In some cases, gas weapons can also be effective. When using aerosol sprays, remember not to stand upwind during deployment, as you might end up affecting yourself rather than your attacker. Telescopic batons are also a good and compact self-defense tool. The choice of suitable self-defense tools should be made individually based on your preferences and local laws and regulations.

WHAT IF THERE'S A SHORTAGE OF BASIC GOODS IN STORES?

We've seen such situations in the history of Poland. Food rationing and empty store shelves. Even in recent times, we witnessed battles in supermarkets over toilet paper. What good is having money if there's a shortage of goods? These situations are usually temporary. Besides, the market doesn't like a vacuum. Desired goods quickly appear on the black market. Of course, you'll have to pay a premium for them, but with the right resources, you can afford it.

The best solution in such a situation is self-sufficiency. This is another reason why it's worth investing in agricultural or recreational land, especially if you don't have your own backyard garden. On such land, you can grow potatoes, cucumbers, tomatoes, and other vegetables, and even grains to help you survive tough times. Even if there's no shortage in stores, food from your own crops is undoubtedly much healthier than that from the market, which is grown on large plantations using artificial fertilizers and pesticides that are not good for our health. Additionally, it saves money, allowing you to build your financial cushion faster.

But what if you don't have land and can't afford to buy it right now, and you live in an apartment building? If you have a balcony, you can turn it into a small garden. Just frame its edges with boards and fill the interior with soil. This way, you can create small beds where you can plant your vegetables. In the case of a building with a flat roof, you can also try to get your neighbors' consent to create a small rooftop garden. Fresh, organic vegetables can be a good bargaining chip. Another idea for partially becoming less dependent on mass food distribution is to create a network of small food producers who supply each other. For example, one person has a vegetable garden, another bakes bread, and a third has a smokehouse and produces meat products. These individuals can collaborate and conduct internal exchanges of goods, ensuring that none of them lacks healthy and diverse food.

WHAT IF THE POWER GOES OUT?

Few people realize the real consequences of a prolonged blackout, or the restriction of access to electrical energy over time, also known as a blackout. Some downplay the problem, while others predict total apocalypse. Of course, everything depends on how long the power outage lasts and in which season it occurs.

In the case of a one-day blackout during the summer, we would mostly face inconvenience. At night, we would have to use candles or battery-powered lamps. We'd have a break from the internet and television, which might actually benefit most of society. The significant inconvenience would be the inability to make purchases since payment terminals and banking systems would not work. Worse yet, cash registers would not work either, so large stores would likely close. Fortunately, small shop owners would probably continue cash sales, recording them on paper for later accounting. However, over time, due to reduced competition, prices might temporarily rise. Many goods would quickly run out, and some would spoil due to a lack of refrigeration. In areas where there are no open stores, there could be riots and looting of closed stores. Therefore, it's always good to have some basic supplies and cash that you can use to buy necessary items. If such a situation were to occur in the summer, it would be worthwhile to prepare a small cellar to store perishable food items from non-functioning refrigerators. In addition to food supplies, having candles, oil lamps, and lanterns with spare batteries is essential. No one knows how long such a power outage could last, so it's crucial to conserve all sources of light and energy. Ideally, owning a personal energy generator is the best solution for a blackout, but not everyone can afford this luxury.

What will definitely not happen in the case of a short blackout?

Financial systems, cryptocurrencies, and the internet will not collapse. The virtual world is decentralized and protected by numerous secure data centers, so our money and data are unlikely to disappear. However, they may not be of much use until the crisis is resolved.

But what if we were without power for several weeks or even months? In such a scenario, there would quickly be unimaginable social and economic changes in every aspect of life, potentially setting us back to the 19th century or worse. It's challenging to prepare for such a situation, so the best survival method is flexibility and the ability to adapt to the prevailing conditions. Fortunately, such a scenario is highly unlikely and would likely be associated with other factors, such as a global natural catastrophe or nuclear war. In such a case, the lack of electrical energy might be the least of our concerns.

WHAT IF CASH COMPLETELY LOSES ITS VALUE?

We are increasingly approaching post-apocalyptic scenarios. Imagine that the global economy has completely collapsed, and nations around the world have lost their authority and credibility. Currently, all world currencies are no longer backed by physical assets like gold but rely solely on the credibility of their issuers, individual nations. What happens when trust in government structures falls to zero? The natural consequence of such a scenario would be the devaluation of currencies to zero. If this catastrophe is not accompanied by the collapse of the internet, cryptocurrencies might take on the role of money. Otherwise, we might resort to barter and a return to real forms of money, such as gold and silver. Copper alloy coins may retain some value as well. Gold coins, due to their high value, may not be suitable for everyday transactions, but silver coins could quickly become a common medium of exchange. This is because of their diversity. In addition to standard one-ounce coins (31.1g), there are various collector's coins and medals weighing 20 and 15 grams. Add to that old circulation coins like Poland's PRL-era "mapki" and "olimpiady" or American silver 25 and 50 cent pieces. With such coins, you could pay for daily purchases or small services. Those who possess such coins will have an advantage. So, as mentioned earlier, silver will not only help preserve the value of our savings during accelerating inflation but also assist us during more apocalyptic scenarios.

WHAT IF THERE'S AN EPIDEMIC?

Despite the COVID-19 pandemic in 2020 turning out to be less severe than initially feared, it raises important questions. What if a truly dangerous virus emerges globally? Many indications suggest that some countries, and possibly even corporations and terrorist organizations, are currently developing advanced biological weapons. Such weapons are ideally designed to target individuals with specific genetic codes while remaining neutral to the rest of the population. Creating such an intelligent virus is not easy, and there are numerous risks associated with such research, including accidental release from the laboratory. How can we protect ourselves in such a situation? Unfortunately, some matters are beyond our control. History has seen many devastating epidemics, with perhaps the worst being the Black Death that swept through Europe in the 14th century.

In some regions, it claimed around 80% of the population. However, despite the lack of antibiotics and low levels of hygiene, about 20% of the population survived. It appears that these survivors owed their health and lives to robust immune systems. Most of those who survived were strong, young, and well-nourished individuals. It was their diet, combined with physical activity, that played a crucial role in their immunity, which lies in the gut.

Much has been written about healthy eating and supplementation, but it's essential to note that maintaining certain healthy habits can significantly increase the likelihood of survival, even during the most significant epidemics.

There's no doubt that fasting has a positive effect on the immune system. Short periods of fasting (up to 48 hours) are especially effective. The most effective of these is water fasting, but one can also try juice fasting. When fasting, the body, no longer digesting food, redirects energy to repairing cells and removing toxins. This kind of regeneration is essential during an epidemic. Fasting not only gives the body a break from processing food but also allows it to rebuild and strengthen its immune system. It's also a good idea to avoid unhealthy foods and highly processed products. It's well known that sugar reduces the efficiency of white blood cells, which are responsible for detecting and neutralizing harmful bacteria and viruses. Therefore, it's essential to eliminate or limit sweets during an epidemic.

Our gut microbiome plays a significant role in the functioning of our immune system. Maintaining a proper balance between "good" and "bad" bacteria is crucial. Regularly consuming foods containing probiotics, such as yogurt, kefir, kimchi, and sauerkraut, can help maintain this balance. Additionally, prebiotic foods like garlic, onions, leeks, and asparagus can nourish the beneficial bacteria in our gut. Proper hydration is also crucial for maintaining a healthy immune system. Water helps flush toxins from our bodies and supports overall cellular function.

Stress and anxiety can weaken our immune system. During an epidemic, it's crucial to manage stress through relaxation techniques like meditation, yoga, or deep breathing exercises. Adequate sleep is also essential for a healthy immune system. Aim for 7-9 hours of quality sleep per night to ensure your body has the opportunity to repair and regenerate.

Finally, consider supplementing your diet with vitamins and minerals that are known to support the immune system, such as vitamin C, vitamin D, zinc, and echinacea. However, it's always best to consult with a healthcare professional before starting any new supplement regimen.

In conclusion, while we can't control the emergence of epidemics or pandemics, we can take steps to strengthen our immune systems and improve our overall health to increase our chances of surviving and staying healthy in the face of infectious diseases

HOW NOT TO FALL VICTIM MEDIA MANIPULATION?

Here, we slowly approach the zombie apocalypse. Why? We'll get to that in a moment.

On October 30, 1938, the entire United States fell into panic due to a Martian invasion scare. This panic was caused by a radio drama adaptation of H.G. Wells' "War of the Worlds." The radio broadcast was so convincing that a significant portion of the audience took it as a real-time account of an ongoing alien invasion. This fascinating phenomenon was thoroughly analyzed by the Rockefeller Foundation, and the lessons drawn from that analysis are still used today in shaping media narratives. As a result, media has the power to manipulate the emotions and moods of entire societies. If people could be convinced of something as unbelievable as a Martian attack in the late 1930s, it's even easier to present real events in a certain light to evoke desired reactions from the audience. Another weapon in the manipulators' arsenal is slowly becoming artificial intelligence, which can generate convincing fake recordings depicting events that never happened or false statements by public figures.

Now, let's return to the analogy of the zombie apocalypse. All-pervasive media controlled by governments and international corporations have the potential to turn entire societies into radio and television-controlled zombies. Those who don't succumb to this narrative can easily be portrayed as public enemies, antisocial individuals, hostile agents of influence, or simply ordinary lunatics. In the realization of the vision of a totalitarian world where media zombies replace oppressive state authorities in pacifying dissenters, technology such as microchip implants combined with fast 5G internet may play a significant role. It would enable total surveillance of every individual and the allocation of points to people, the lack of which could effectively hinder one's life or even exclude them from society. For example, if you're disobedient, you won't get credit, find a job, or get your child into college. Such soft repression mechanisms can be virtually limitless, with contemporary China serving as a prominent example.

The most recent example of such actions are the restrictions imposed by governments around the world in response to the COVID-19 pandemic. I won't analyze the validity of these government actions here; I'll just present the mechanisms used to enforce compliance. Some governments resorted to traditional police force, while others focused on more modern methods. I'll use the actions of the Polish government, which I observed daily, as an example. Firstly, the alleged pandemic became the main topic in all media outlets. News constantly reported the current number of infections, primarily driven by an increase in testing. Simultaneously, no one informed us about the true health status of those infected and the significant margin of error in PCR tests. Severe cases were highlighted to subconsciously make us consider such disease progression as typical. At the same time, the scapegoats of this crisis were presented to us: those who resisted sanitary regulations. Among them, individuals refusing to wear masks were most prominently condemned. They were portrayed as irresponsible egoists who deserved "infamy" and posed a threat to society. These hate campaigns made individuals resisting restrictions more fearful of their fellow citizens' reactions than the potential fines, leading to various forms of unpleasantness, from verbal attacks to restricted access to goods and services, to physical violence. So, what can we do about this? First and foremost, don't approach media information emotionally. Observe your immediate surroundings and ask yourself if what you're hearing really happens. Seek information on a given topic from independent online sources, but remember to critically assess their credibility. Just because a source is independent doesn't always mean it's right or telling the truth. Above all, keep thinking and rely on reason and experience rather than emotions. Experience is particularly important. Society's political memory typically extends no further than 1.5 years back. So, look for historical analogies and analyze them in light of the media information at the time versus the actual situation, which becomes clearer with time. Sometimes, it's worth going on a low-information diet – turn off the TV, disconnect from the internet, don't read newspapers, and start forming your perception of the world based solely on your observations. Share these methods and your thoughts with others. The smaller the portion of society that succumbs to manipulation, the greater the chance of living in a truly free world.

FIGHTING WITH AN OPEN VISOR OR GOING UNDERGROUND?

First, we must ask ourselves whether to engage in the fight at all. The primary focus of this analysis is survival, and engaging in a fight can always result in defeat. Remember that survival is not always the ultimate goal. Throughout history, people have sacrificed their lives and health in the name of higher ideals or to ensure the safety of their loved ones. Undoubtedly, there are causes in this world worth paying the highest price for, and everyone can identify them based on their own values. However, we should not rashly sacrifice our lives, health, or property. As General Patton once said, "The object of war is not to die for your country but to make the other bastard die for his." So, we must carefully assess the risks of engaging in a fight and whether this is the right moment. In Polish history, there have been many failed national uprisings, from the Bar Confederation to the January and November Uprisings, to the tragic Warsaw Uprising. In hindsight, many of these uprisings can be seen as unnecessary sacrifices of blood that weakened our nation and worsened the political situation. When deciding to fight, we must consider the possible consequences of potential defeat. Sometimes it is better to wait for a favorable moment when the enemy is weakened or preoccupied with other matters, and our forces and resources are stronger. This is precisely what happened during the successful Greater Poland Uprising, which began in 1918 and 1919 when the German occupier was weakened after the defeat in the just-concluded World War I. The material and ideological preparations for this national uprising took more than 50 years, and when combined with the opportune historical moment, it resulted in a spectacular victory over an enemy that had appeared invincible just a few years earlier. When faced with the choice of whether to fight, we should think rationally about our chances of victory and about protecting our loved ones as a top priority. Sometimes, going underground and into hiding may be the best solution. Although it doesn't involve open combat, it represents passive resistance to the enemy. We can still sabotage their actions and organize underground networks. Such actions allow us to maintain relative safety while not submitting to the surrounding tyranny. It also provides an opportunity to pass on our values to future generations and empower them to act when the time is right.

However, everything depends on the political and geopolitical situation, whether we are fighting against an occupier or oppressor or a domestic tyranny and totalitarianism. One certainty is that we should not fight alone. Some form of larger organization is necessary, with trusted friends who share common interests and values. Unity is strength!

WHAT ABOUT A CLASSIC KINETIC WAR?

Many people believe that traditional kinetic wars are a thing of the past, and it might seem that a global conflict like World War III is unlikely. A global kinetic conflict is not in anyone's interest, and its role has currently been taken over by the global information war. However, local conflicts are still happening, where major players manipulate events behind the scenes to protect their own territory from the chaos of war. Poland's geopolitical position unfortunately means that it could become a theater for such a local armed conflict. I won't delve into who might be involved in such a conflict, but I'll focus on what to do to find one's way through it and survive, regardless of one's geographic location. I assume that the reader is not a professional soldier or a member of a territorial defense force but a civilian responsible for their property and family.

As history teaches us, mass civilian exoduses accompany all armed conflicts. We've all seen long columns of refugees in movies, dragging their belongings along the roads, often targeted by enemy aircraft. Today, it's unlikely that people will flee on foot; instead, we may see congested roads and highways. In the event of a real threat of war in our region, it will be essential to have a fully fueled vehicle. It's also wise to have a reserve of fuel, just in case. Ensure that your vehicle carries essential survival items, such as food supplies and warm clothing. If possible, pack everything you would like to take with you in case you need to leave. Money and valuable items like gold and silver coins should be well-hidden in your luggage, making sure to stash them in different places to prevent the loss of all your resources. Check if it's possible to leave your location using less crowded, less traveled roads to avoid traffic jams and potential problems. Be prepared to travel on foot if necessary. However, fleeing should be considered a last resort. Your home is part of your assets that you want to protect, and it also provides shelter from the elements. By staying at home, you remain inconspicuous and avoid provoking potential attacks. In the event of a war, those living outside the cities may be in a somewhat better position. It is highly likely that combat will focus on major cities because controlling cities automatically guarantees control over nearby rural areas. Therefore, it's a good idea to have the option to escape beyond the city limits, whether to your recreational property or to family or friends. In such a place, you have a better chance of weathering the worst times until the situation stabilizes. During a war, it's also good to have some form of weaponry. Keep in mind that the period of chaos during a war is a haven for all sorts of criminals and degenerates you may need to defend yourself and your loved ones against. Black powder firearms can be highly effective in such situations. If the opportunity arises, consider upgrading to more modern weapons. Firearms can also serve for hunting. Once you've retreated to a rural area, all the aforementioned precautions will help you. An essential aspect of survival is having a source of food. To survive for an extended period, it's essential to be self-sufficient with a vegetable garden that provides at least partial food self-sufficiency. Silver coins may also come in handy in times of crisis when local currency is no longer accepted. American dollars or the currency of another politically and economically stable country can also play a similar role. In such circumstances, you should be able to endure a relatively short local conflict and provide relative safety for yourself and your loved ones.

ZOMBIE APOCALYPSE!

Now, we've arrived at the eagerly awaited zombie apocalypse. I know some readers might be disappointed, but I'll approach this concept symbolically. These zombies won't be living corpses feasting on brains, at least not in the literal sense. Our zombies will be the majority of society who have fallen prey to mass media propaganda. People controlled by hate-filled broadcasts from mainstream news stations. Perhaps, in the near future, mass manipulation will reach even higher levels.

I foresee two scenarios. The first is connected to a global system of social control based on monitoring and surveillance, linked by a superfast internet and analyzed by supercomputers. This system will know almost everything about us and will reward or punish us based on that data. The system of rewards and punishments may also encourage people to report on others. For example, if you report on your neighbor, we'll lower your mortgage rate or give you extra vacation days.

The second scenario, not mutually exclusive with the first, involves implanting chips in most of the population to monitor our location, health, and even our feelings. Perhaps technology will allow for direct control of our moods and even thoughts through these chips. In this dark scenario, most people will become cogs in a system they don't even realize is controlling them, unable to resist. Such a system will likely encourage citizens to snitch on each other. If you don't conform, you might not get a job or access to credit. One control mechanism could be the introduction of a universal basic income, a sum of money paid to every citizen. If you don't achieve financial independence, you may be easily coerced into collaboration with the system. This control could extend to tracking every aspect of our lives, including our location, health, and even emotions through implanted chips. Unfortunately, such scenarios are becoming increasingly likely, with early signs of them appearing in countries like China. It's in our best interest to try to stop this systemic zombification through active and passive resistance against the ambitions of those in power and by raising awareness among the population. But what if such scenarios become a reality in the future?

First and foremost, we must do everything to avoid becoming part of the system. Escaping from it could involve moving out of city centers, which will be the first areas to become part of this grand experiment. Financial independence is crucial, as those who don't comply may be denied jobs or access to credit. Some form of new identification might even be tied to your mobile device, making it hard to avoid carrying it. In such a situation, a Faraday cage could help. This cage would block your device from transmitting data about your location, allowing you to move outside the system's control.

The greater challenge might be the implanted chips. Perhaps specialists will find ways to hack these chips to regain control over their functions. However, it's best to do everything to avoid having such devices implanted. Unfortunately, this might lead to a life outside society and possibly outside the law. It may deprive you of the ability to earn a living, access healthcare, education, and any form of state protection. This is already hinted at with vaccine passports or COVID certificates, available only to vaccinated individuals.

People wishing to maintain their freedom may have to live in isolation from society, creating communities that operate according to pre-industrial principles. These communities must be self-sufficient, with economic activity limited to members of the local community or similar communities nearby.

There will likely also be a black market. Some individuals or groups living within the system may find a way to break free and engage in illegal activities with residents of non-system communities. Such contacts can provide city residents with access to healthy, unprocessed food and residents of non-system communities with access to modern technology. Such interactions may force residents of non-system communities to venture into urban areas, which can be fraught with danger, not only from government repression but also from indoctrinated city dwellers who may perceive outsiders as a threat to their security and welfare.

In this situation, you will need appropriate camouflage. Participants in such expeditions will need to blend in with city residents in appearance and may also need fake digital certificates. It's hard to predict what form these solutions might take, but human creativity is boundless. Non-system communities will also need some form of defense, as they may encounter various criminals living off theft and terrorizing vulnerable, unprotected communities. Less concern should be given to attacks from the system. It probably won't see small communities living on the fringes of civilization as significant threats, provided they don't infiltrate the zombified population.

CONCLUSION

As you can see, possessing a certain set of knowledge, skills, and competencies can help you survive in many challenging situations. All the components of this set of skills intersect with each other. Once you acquire them, you become versatile individuals capable of handling most difficult situations. Many other crisis scenarios can be imagined that I haven't covered here. However, I believe that by remembering the principles outlined above, you can cope with all of them without losing hope or succumbing to despair. So, let's be sensible and effective in our actions. Remember that after every night, a new day always brings hope for a better tomorrow.

www.ingramcontent.com/pod-product-compliance
Lightning Source LLC
Chambersburg PA
CBHW071001290526
45795CB00005B/1733